GAIL CROWDER
AND OTHER SEXY WIVES

Published by G.A.I.L Publishing LLC

Copyright 2011© by Gail Crowder and Other Sexy Wives.
All rights reserved. No part of this book may be reproduced, photocopying, stored in a retrieval system or transmitted in any form by any means without the prior written permission of the publisher.

Cover Photograph
Cindy Alderton | Boudoir Affaire Photography

Book Cover and book layout by
Anita Gillespie-Luckett | Anita's Designs & Events

Edited by Dieneke Johnson
Edited by Ms. Sunkist

Published by G.A.I.L Publishing LLC
www.bringingitbacktothemarriage.com
www.bsbconference.com
301-646-1259
ISBN-13: 978-0-9832185-0-0

Logo design by Marie Mickle

Editorial content submitted by women across America and Canada. Release form signed for content release.

Disclaimer
Certain suggestions are made in this book. While these are intended to be helpful to the reader, the reader must assume all risk associated with following any particular suggestion. Therefore, in purchasing this book, the reader agrees that the authors and publisher are not liable or responsible for any injury or damaged caused by the use of any information contained herein.

All of the characters in this book are based on real persons, but in some cases, names have been omitted or changed to protect the privacy of the people involved. Therefore, any resemblance to actual persons, living or dead is purely coincidental, unless authorized by the actual person mentioned.

Printed in the United States of America

Acknowledgements

I would like to thank my Lord and Savior, Jesus Christ, for giving me this creative mind, and for allowing me to walk out this predestined journey. To my husband Gil, my friend, my lover, and my sounding board; I thank you for being the man of God that you were called to be, and for allowing me to be just me. To my two sons, Justin and Joshua; Mommy loves you more than life. To my mother, Sharron J. White; thank you so much for believing in me when I didn't believe in myself, and for helping to finance the dream that lives inside me. I am forever grateful. To my Dad Larry P. White thanks so much for allowing me to talk for hours on the phone with you about my dreams for my business. To my Aunt Clarice B. Jackson; thanks for teaching me your grace and elegance. You are truly timeless.

To my sisters not by birth but by spirit -- Joy, Val, Kim, Judy and Chrystal -- thank you for being a pain in my-you-know-what? (Smile) For your prayers, your laughs, your tears, your ideas, your phone calls, your support, your helping hands and your love, I am truly grateful. Thank you, thank you!

To Anita Gillespie-Luckett and Marie Mickle, two of the best graphic artists in the business; I thank you for your time, your creativity, and for helping me get what's in my head and what I see in my dreams onto paper! To Dieneke Johnson; thank you so much for making me look good on paper. To Cindy Alderton, all I can say: Girl, you make me shine on film!

To all the ladies from all across the United States and the world who sent their story submissions; without you this book wouldn't be possible. To sexy and potential wives who purchase this book; I pray that you find a tip, a story or an idea that will enhance and enrich your marriage to take it to the next level.

To all the ladies who work hard at the BSB Conference to ensure that the ladies who attend have a good time! I thank you from the bottom of my heart! God Bless you.

With love,

Hail

Introduction

From one "Sexy Wife" to another:

Some of you will read this book and will come away with fresh new ideas. You and your spouse may become more willing to introduce new ideas and approaches into your bedroom. Others will walk away merely entertained. Whichever your experience, it is my heart's desire that you walk away with an open mind, and the hope that you too can have a hot and passionate love life within the intimacy of your marriage.

God created marriage and decreed that the marriage bed is honorable in all, and the bed undefiled (**Hebrews 13:4**). So as you read the real life stories of each Sexy Wife, just know that passion and creativity can be yours within your own marriage.

Table of Contents

The Panty Droppa	1
Happy Endings	5
Ways to Keep the Fire Alive	11
Penelope	15
Romance for Life	20
The Challenge	24
How to Become a Sexy Wife	29
These Last Words	32
Celebrating Our Engagement	37
Foreplay	41
First Encounter	44
Rewind	50

The Panty Droppa

It was an early Friday evening and we both had gotten off from work not long ago. Dusk blanketed the sky, revealing little sprinkles of stars and clouds. The roads were fairly quiet with the exception of a few cars here and there zipping through the park that we chose as our destination. We sat across from each other in the front of my cherry-red tinted out *Volvo*; he in the passenger's seat and I in the driver's. Trey Songz's *Panty Droppa* vibrated through the speakers; the sound of his deep sultry voice caused my juices to flow and my panties to stain. As I glanced over at Lamar and took a quick peek at his thick sexy lips and muscular arms protruding through the grey Polo sweater he was wearing, I clenched the steering wheel, leaving a slight indention with my fingernails. He gently pulled my hand away from the steering wheel towards him, kissing it ever so sweetly. The softness of his lips along with the roughness of his beard against my hand caused my thighs to quiver. My nipples ripened as he slid my index finger inside his hot wet mouth and sucked it. He bit on his bottom lip and leaned over the console, cupping my face with his big bear-paw hands. Lamar kissed me fervently on the lips, intertwining my tongue with his. He caressed my face and ran his fingers through my short curly hair. We came to a short pause; I looked into his hazel colored puppy dog eyes, which were overwhelmed with love and passion. He bit his lip again, enticing me in such a way that I found myself climbing into the passenger seat with him and landing on his lap.

He wrapped his burly arms around my body, grasping my size DD chest in his hands as if they were two mini basketballs. He pinched my nipples through my blouse, causing me to moan lightly.

"You like that baby?" Lamar asked, biting at the nape of my neck.

"Yes, baby." I answered breathlessly, planting my petite hands on top of his.

I threw my head back and closed my eyes as his tongue traveled from my neck to my ear.

The heat from his breath caused goose bumps to cover my body. I could feel his hard-on pressing through his jeans. I unzipped his pants and slid my hand through the opening, releasing his growing manhood. I licked my thumb and then circled the tip of his hardened rod.

Lamar gripped my waist as I continued to massage his member with my hand. He wrestled with the clasp on my trousers, eventually unsnapping them. He then fiddled with the buttons on my blouse with his gigantic fingers. After unbuttoning two of the buttons, he ripped my shirt open effortlessly, causing the rest of them to pop off, revealing my lacey black demi cupped bra. I shimmied my pants down to the floor and lifted my body up slightly so he could do the same.

He pushed my panties to the side and entered me forcefully from behind. I danced around in his lap in short rhythmic motions as he grabbed at my body like an octopus. We moaned together as we swayed to the beat of the *Panty Droppa* song which was now on repeat. The thrill of being in the car took over my body, causing my juices to slither down his hardened member. He held me close as he wrapped his hand around to the opening between my legs. He pried my lips apart like a burglar breaking into a well armed house Ad petted my kitty until I began to purr.

"Oh baby, faster" I whispered gyrating my hips from side to side.

"Tell daddy how good it is?" He demanded as he threw my frame against his lap over and over again.

"It's yours, daddy!" I squealed, gripping the dashboard as he pushed his manhood deeper inside.

He continued stroking my kitty and bouncing me up and down on his lap, causing us both to let out loud moans and groans of pure pleasure that only we could share together. The windows fogged as we continued going at each other like two animals in heat. Sweat dripped from our bodies as we climbed to a level of heightened pleasure that caused me to feel like heaven was only a grasp away. As we climaxed together, something we had never done before, it was clear that our love for each other, after all of these years, was so very true that nothing could ever take it away.

"Damn baby, that was good." Lamar said taking a long, deep breath. "I love you, girl."

"I love you too, baby." I said, turning and kissing him on the lips. "I love you too."

Happy Endings

The plane ride to Africa was exhausting! I endured eighteen hours in the air, an hour layover in Rome, a major case of insomnia that left me eager to get off Ethiopian Air - Flight 1618. Once off the plane, I was greeted by a tall, creamy toned, statuesque Ethiopian Air employee with warm almond shaped eyes. He flashed me a smile (that included a beautiful set of straight, white teeth) and said, "Welcome Home, My Sister!" At that moment, an indescribable sense of belonging overcame me. I WAS home!

I made it to the Hilton Hotel in Ethiopia's capital, Addis Ababa, without incident and settled in.

Gail Crowder and Other Sexy Wives

After checking in and taking a much needed nap, I decided to tour the hotel before meeting up with my colleagues for dinner. The hotel and grounds were absolutely magnificent. It had twenty store-front shops, a beauty/barber salon, three restaurants, indoor and outdoor pools and a large vestibule with exotic flowers, birds and trees. The air was resplendent with peace and serenity. The Ethiopian people were exceptionally gracious, welcoming and willing to share their last. I truly experienced love.

At the time, I worked for the Center for Disease Control (CDC) out of Atlanta, GA. My colleagues and I were there for the grand opening of the newest, state-of-the-art hospital that had been recently constructed. We shared this memorable event with some of the most influential contractors, philanthropists, investors, diplomats, Sheiks, lawyers, doctors, leaders and celebrities from around the world. We were going to be in Africa for an entire week, and four of the seven days were dedicated solely to hospital events and meetings. The other three were reserved for shopping, sightseeing, relaxing and more shopping! By day four, I was so worn out that after the day's festivities I opted to have a drink at the bar. I ordered a shot of Patrone and a St. George's. St. George's is the local beer that is served in a tall glass that appears to hold the equivalent of forty ounces. I sat at the bar for at least an hour enjoying the remarkable house band that was performing and was told that they were from Virginia, USA. Longing for "normal conversation," I had an opportunity to talk about something other than business with the band members and other hotel guests. While getting tipsy, I also met some distinguished photographers, pilots and ambassadors. The bartender was a handsome Ethiopian by the name of Solomon. We engaged in some small talk about the band, entertainers that frequented the hotel and the "must see" sites. He commented on how exhausted I looked and reminded me to visit the hotel's spa. I was so glad that he mentioned it, because I had completely forgotten about that amenity. A soothing Swedish Massage was exactly what I needed to get to that tranquil, calming place for which I yearned. After leaving the bar, I strolled to the spa to make my appointment. I reserved an appointment for the following afternoon, and then took my inebriated self to bed.

The next day I awoke feeling surprisingly refreshed and energized. After ordering a small omelet, toast and juice from room service, I got dressed and caught a taxi to the Post Office, a popular shopping district. I wanted to buy everything I saw! The artwork, sculptures and jewelry were absolutely stunning. After spending all of the money budgeted for that outing, I returned to the hotel to prepare for my spa treatment. Upon arrival, my olfactory nerve was immediately met by the splendid assortment of aromas of lemon grass, lavender, eucalyptus and roses. Sade's "Diamond Life" resounded softly and sweetly in the background. Once I signed in, my assigned masseuse escorted me to one of the spacious massage rooms. He asked me to disrobe and lie down on the massage table face down. I stood there patiently waiting expecting him to exit the room so that I could get undressed. When he didn't budge, noticing my expression, he explained that it was customary for the therapist to remain in the room, but if I felt more comfortable with him not being there, he'd be more than happy to leave. I figured I'd go with the flow and just let it all hang out (thanks to gravity). As I got onto the table, I had this eerie suspicion that his eyes were glued to my butt. He quickly got to business and covered me partially with a sheet. He asked what type of aromatherapy I preferred and I settled for eucalyptus. He performed his magic on my back, neck, derriere and legs. My miracle worker then requested that I turn over onto my back. I happily obliged and he massaged my feet and legs. Once he reached my torso, he asked me if I would like for him to massage my stomach. I had experienced this type of abdominal manipulation technique only once before, because of some digestive issues I had in the past, and at that point I was willing to allow him to massage anything he could find on my body. I was relaxed and feeling so phenomenal that I could have gone to sleep right there. As my stomach massage ensued, a tingly, unusual (well unusual for that atmosphere) feeling overcame me and before I knew it, I was having an orgasm, right there on the massage table! It happened so quickly that all I could do was try to calm myself, in hopes that he did not sense my heavy breathing and body convulsions. He was professional and acted as if he knew nothing, which eased my mind, but only a little. "Oh my, what just happened?", "Does he know?", and "Is this considered cheating?" ran through my mind all at once. After working on my stomach, he moved up to my breasts and caressed them like I never knew possible. He was still very much professional, but I was beginning to think that this was not the typical massage session. By the time he was done, I wanted to pack him up in my bag and take him back to Atlanta. I had never felt so soothed, tranquil, and --most of all-- pleased. I left my new best friend a tip that far surpassed the price of the actual massage. I seemed to float back up to my room. When I opened the door, I was prepared to take a long, luxurious bath, but was instead met at the door by my sexy husband. What a startling yet incredible surprise! The CDC surprised us by flying our spouses to Africa to share in the splendid experience. I was still on my orgasm high and seeing my "Honey" that I missed so much only intensified my horniness. We shared a passionate kiss that seemed endless and resulted in my attempting to rip off every piece of clothing he had on. "Honey" gave me a look of pure confusion, as I'm sure he wondered what had gotten into me. I just gave him an assuring smile as I stripped him naked. I stood at the foot of the bed and just looked him over; thanking God for the marvel he made especially for me. After taking him in visually, I knelt down in front of him and licked him from the inside of his thigh, along the outside of his hip, to the middle of his torso, past his belly button, up his chest, to his chin where I finally licked around his lips-- all while removing my clothing except for my black, lacy thong. I took his bottom lip and sucked it with urgency and determination. I moaned as he gently caressed my back and ran his fingers through my hair. My body wanted him so badly and he could tell by my protruding nipples and moist center that "it was on"! We kissed some more and I turned my attention back to his body. I moved down to his nipples and began to lick and gently nibble at them. As I witnessed his excitement rise, I moved down to his long, thick appendage. I turned my body around and situated myself in the 6-9 position. I teased and pleased him until it looked like he was having a seizure. "Honey" added a clitoral orgasm to the growing list of orgasms I had accumulated thus far and I was again satisfied. He was far from done with me though. He slapped it, flipped it, rubbed it down, pulled my hair and turned me every which way but loose in that room. We continued to pleasure each other for the better half of the early evening. I am proud to say that I was also able to get my vaginal orgasm in before we were done! Here's to TWO (or more) HAPPY ENDINGS in one day!

Ways to Keep the Fire Alive

Many years ago I found myself in a tough spot. We had been married for a while, and my husband and I didn't want any more children. BUT he refused to get a vasectomy, and I couldn't always remember to take my birth control; so there we were. I tried different methods and nothing seemed to fit. Then my doctor informed me of Depo-Provera. It is a shot that you get four times a year to prevent pregnancy. So I thought, why not give it a try? And that's just what I did.

What the doctor didn't tell me is that it would KILL my sex drive. And I don't mean slightly lower, I mean it KILLED it! It also affected my natural lubrication. I went from wanting to have sex every other night to not wanting it at all. It was absolutely horrifying and frustrating. It felt like my body was turning on me. And when you're 24 years old and your sex drive has left and no one tells you what to do, you feel lost. I had no idea that there were so many things that could help. As I worked my way through this challenge, I learned many ways to naturally increase my desire. Know that if your sex drive changes there is no shame AND it may take a little more work to get aroused than it did in the past. With that being said, here are a few things that I found helpful. I hope it helps!

- Think of yourself as sexy. Remember you are a sexual creature. Build yourself up throughout the day. Make a conscious effort to stay in touch with your sexiness. Gently touch your neck, swing your hair or do whatever reminds you that you are a sensual creature.

- Plan a night of intimacy. It might not feel as romantic but if you need time to prepare mentally, physically and spiritually, setting aside time in advance can help. Now, be careful not to schedule your lovin' time like a chore. Remember this is a special time you're setting aside, not a duty to perform. Make it something to look forward to.

- Have a dirty talk or send a sexy text or email to your husband.

- Get a book of erotica. Now this was very helpful. Reading an erotic story beforehand helps to get the energy flowing. Getting the fire started before the hubby gets there goes a long way.

- Speaking of erotica; spend some time with yourself and put your hand on YOURSELF. During that time I found that I needed more stimulation in some areas and less in others. That way I could tell the hubbub exactly where and how to touch me.

- Get some toys. You may want to invest in some sex toys that you and the hubby can use together. A cock ring with a vibrating bullet can add quite a bit of spice. Or vibrating panties with a remote (which your husband gets to control) is a fun one too! Don't be shy, you can go online and order them and no one has to know.

- Speaking of toys, let's look at ointments and lubes. Now clitoral stimulation creams and a little lube go a long way here. Especially if you are not producing as much natural lubricant (a side effect of Depo-Provera). Flavored lube is also nice. A good G-spot stimulator cream can go a long way as well.

- Experiment with new things. Try giving each other a massage, whips, blindfolds, hand cuffs or a feather.

- Now on a practical note, consider removing your TV from the bedroom. I know it sounds crazy BUT removing the TV helped my mind and body to remember that the bed is for two things: sleeping and sex!

Remember all of these things are just suggestions, and you can mix and match them to create the experience you want. Just know that you are not alone. With some patience and a little creativity, you can have an exciting sex life again!

Penelope

As I stand in this bathroom, I can't believe what I am doing; purple wig... sexy red lipstick... my new cashmere perfume sprayed in all of the right places... Oh yeah, and don't forget a nightie and heels that I stashed under the sink specifically for this occasion...Well, here goes nothing!

My husband is a wonderful man. He is always trying new tricks and techniques to keep me pleased in the bedroom. Sometimes I feel bad because in all honesty... I am extremely lazy! Now, don't get me wrong, I alternate between positions and embark on kinky "Roller Coaster" type activities that my husband enjoys every now and then - I just don't particularly tend to "create" new techniques like my husband does... It's so cliché to start a story with "one day" but that's literally how the idea came to me!

"One day" as I was sitting at my desk, I had the brilliant idea of creating an alternate bedroom personality. I didn't exactly know what the personality would look like, but I did know that I wanted her to be something that I wasn't in the bedroom; creative, wild, and CRAZY! Someone who wouldn't be afraid to be "creative" and who wouldn't feel bashful over what had taken place the next day. I knew that she had to look completely different from me on the outside and truly think and feel differently from within. She would also only be allowed to come out for bedroom play. Ohhhhhh yes, I had it all figured out! Complete with my thoughts and ideas, I dragged my girlfriend to the local "naughty" store and bought a purple wig and stark red lipstick. I paired the wig and lipstick with a new black nightie, red high heels, and new cashmere scented perfume. With all of these items, I just KNEW that I was ready to bring my alternate personality to fruition and simply only needed to give her a name... There is so much that goes into a name. Your name truly determines who you are and what you will be! What in God's name was I going to call this person? Roxie? No...Stacy? No... What was I going to call this personality?? Whatever the name was going to be, it had to be something sexy enough to spark heat at the very thought of it, while remaining discreet enough to be spoken in a room full of professionals. It seemed like destiny when the name finally came to me...Penelope."

With Penelope finally formed, I was ready to go home and "get to work." As soon as I walked in the door, I kissed my husband and walked straight into the bathroom to stash my bag. I hid the bag in the counter under the kitchen sink and proceeded to complete my evening duties: homework with my son – check; dinner made and dishes washed – check; lunch made and stored for work – check; my son bathed and put to bed... check! Now it was time for action! I went into the bathroom and locked the door behind me. I was so nervous that I almost didn't go forward with this new creation. I showered and cleaned every nook and cranny known to man. When I tell you that I was glistening when I emerged from that shower, you'd better believe that I was glistening! When I was finished showering, I proceeded to fix my make-up. For this process, I wanted to channel a sexy superhero! I used the same red lipstick as an eye shadow and put on extra mascara, cat-like eyeliner, and a hint of blush in all of the right places. I then carefully oiled my skin and applied the new perfume to all of my pulse points. Once the "body preparations" were complete, I carefully put on the nightie, high heels, and finally, the purple wig... Show time! With wobbly knees, I stepped out of the bathroom, walked into the bedroom, and flipped the light on. I looked my husband dead in the eye and in my sexiest "Come hither" voice, I said "Your wife has officially left the building; let me introduce you to Penelope." Here is where the story gets interesting... My husband took one look at me, said "Ohhhhhh" and walked towards me. My nervousness was at "full speed"! I pulled my husband into my arms, sexily grabbed and pulled his face towards mine, went in for the kill, and... ... He started laughing hysterically... I mean, he just didn't stop! When he finally pulled himself together, he said "Baby, I'm sorry, I just can't do this – I feel like I am cheating on my wife. Please, take all of that crap off and bring me back my wife."

I am not going to tell you a lie, folks: At first I was a little mad to have spent so much money only to be laughed at, but you know what? Once I took off those heels and all of the make-up was washed from my face, I was grateful for the little piece of normalcy from that crazy evening! I walked back into the room and my husband immediately grabbed me and led me to the bed. He switched from being my gentle giant to being this passionately intense and sexy lover straight out of an old school romance novel! Every twist and turn that he took me on that night felt better than our first time making love. It was as if he was transformed into a Professional love making Super Man whose mission was only to bring both of us to the outer heavens! Before that night, I had only heard stories of multiple, long-lasting orgasms, I hadn't yet experienced them. Needless to say that on that special night... I simply lost count!

Without a doubt, that was the BEST sexual experience that I had ever had in my life and it all happened because of Penelope!

Romance for Life

    Long before I attended the "Bringing Sexy Back" conference I decided to be a sexy wife. And that means practicing these seven rules that I firmly believe will help create "Romance for Life".

1. Place God at the center of your relationship
2. Never stop being beautiful; inside and out
3. Keep the lines of communication open
4. Cook for your man

5. Praise your man
6. Make your home a warm and welcoming retreat
7. Allow for breathing space by doing things alone

Cultivating sexiness in a marriage can include many things; from being mysterious to being assertive or from traveling together to a variety in locations for physical intimacy. We all know that your love life will not stay sexy on its own. There's a lot you can do. For example, try to assess what stage of marriage you are in. My understanding is that there are five stages in marriage... My husband and I are in the last stage (twenty to twenty five years) called the "New Freedom" stage or the final stage, described as a time when couples experience a peaceful understanding. Regardless of what stage you're in, it is vital that all of your efforts are directed toward the each of you growing individually while simultaneously maintaining your marriage.

Here's one example of how I've brought sexy back into my marriage... What I find fascinating about creating moments to lovingly enjoy my husband is that we are currently living in a very exciting, yet content, time in our lives. Exciting because discovery is involved; contentment because I mean--come on people-- it's been 24 years. You see, we're almost empty nesters. Our two young adult children are in their twenties. One has moved out and the other is almost never home. So we're rediscovering our home, our time and our bodies. My most recent sexual escapade with my adorable husband of 24 years began with a dinner date via cell phone-- courtesy of me. In my best "I'm Gonna Get My Man" sultry voice I tickled his ears with flirty talk until we both agreed to meet downtown at our favorite Peruvian restaurant-- you know; the little hole in the wall that's been around for 19 years. It's one of our main rendezvous spots. Over the years we've returned because it's charmingly quaint and one of the few places from our dating years that's still around. Besides, they serve great ceviche and a terrific pisco sour.

We ordered a light meal of soup and appetizers, saving room for desert, because that'll come later. With alluring eyes, we exchanged seductive glances while discussing the events of the day, which slowly evolved into squeezing hands and rubbing arms to even playing footsies under the table (Don't be afraid to get a little silly). Feeling sated but not overly full we strolled arm-in-arm to the car silently, making plans to visit some of the exotic places we passed. Once home we both settled into our regular routine of listening to messages and opening mail. After a short while I put the water on for ginger tea and prepared a tray with mini red velvet cakes from the local bakery and placed it on the dining room table. I then instructed "Mr. HD" to take a break from his laptop when I returned. By then the water would be hot. Meanwhile, I went upstairs to our bedroom and lit a few scented candles, put on some seductive music, showered with my extra favorite shower gel and body cream, slipped on my satin bra set with the satin laced bottom and my black patent leather stilettos. Then I slipped on one his favorite shirts he wears to work. As I walked down the stairs he's unaware of the good time that lies ahead because he's now watching TV. I slowly grabbed the tray of tea and cakes and sauntered over to him, and then asked "See anything you like?" Well, he stared with delight while reaching for the remote to turn off the TV after I placed the tray on the coffee table; I did a seductive dance which led to him kissing my navel and breasts. Then I led him upstairs to our room and—well, let's say the tea got cold by the time we decided to drink it. Whew OMG! We must have tea and cake again real soon. And we did!

The Challenge

My husband and I challenge each other quite often. So much so that even the littlest things become huge, because we keep each other on our toes with the challenges. Needless to say; the same can be said about our sex life.

I was driving one day, thinking about my husband and the little escapade we'd had the night before. My body responded in a way that I hadn't anticipated but I welcomed the feeling. As many would say, I became horny. So I decided to text my husband my latest challenge for him.

I sent him a text saying, "I have a challenge for you." He texted back, "What do you need me to do?" I replied, "I need you to fill all three holes at the same time. If you can do that for me I'll love you for life." He texted back, "I got you!"

The day seemed to drag by. I was anticipating the challenge. I knew exactly what I wanted him to do, but would he know? Yes, it would have been easy to just tell him but we're supposed to know what our partner wants, right? Besides, this was our way of making the world we shared more exciting.

My husband made it home before I did that evening. As I entered the house, nothing seemed out of the ordinary, so I figured he would probably just wait until we were headed to bed before he would do anything special. I walked over to where he sat and gave him a soft kiss on the lips and told him that I missed him. He told me he missed me too. I went into our bedroom and lying on the bed was an envelope. I opened it and inside was a piece of white paper printed from a computer.

It read:

ARREST WARRANT

Execution Date: NOW

A warrant for the arrest of your heart has been issued; due to the fact it now belongs to me, and that you are no longer in control of it, you must be informed of your rights. You have the right to remain silent while you are being kissed and licked, from head to toe, as well as having all orifices filled simultaneously. You also have the right to be still while being bound in four point restraints, and prosecuted by the court of love. You have the right to be ravished in random locations, no matter the time or circumstances. Anything you say, moan or scream during these sexual escapades may be used against you and held in favor of this court of love. Please be advised that once signed, this document will go into effect immediately without further notice.

In the unlikely event that this document is not taken seriously, the court will be forced to plead this case with total unrestrained desire and satisfaction. This will include but not limited to kissing, licking, and sucking until you pass out. The court will blow your mind in every way imaginable for as long as your body can stand it.

Respectfully submitted:

Your husband

The bottom of the letter read:

Your sentence has already been determined. For the best interest of the parties involved, you have been found guilty of love in the first degree. The court demands the maximum sentence. You are sentenced to life without the possibility of parole with ME!

I started to laugh shortly after reading the last line. Smiling, I turned around to find him standing in the doorway.

He walked towards me saying, "So, it's funny." I kept on laughing and said, "No, it was cute."

"Cute, huh? You saw what it said would happen, if you don't take this matter seriously," he said as he grabbed me by my arm, pulling me closer to him.

"Take off your clothes right now!"

I was smiling the whole time but did exactly what he said. I was becoming extremely aroused.

By the time I finished undressing I wanted him so badly, but he was still fully dressed. So I stood there just looking at him. He came over grabbed me by my arm again and spun me around, putting one hand behind my back. I heard a clicking sound as I felt cold metal around my wrist. He then grabbed my other arm, putting the other hand in what I now know were handcuffs. I stood there wondering what he would do next. He started to slowly undress as I stood there watching. It was exciting, to say the least, but frustrating because I wanted to touch him, undress him, make love to him-- but I couldn't do anything because of the restraints. He lay down on the bed.

"Turn around and assume the 69 position," he said.

My heart was racing and I could feel the moisture between my legs building. I climbed on top of him and could feel his manhood pressing up against me. He grabbed my legs and with one quick motion pulled me towards him. As I began to fill one of "my holes" on my own, he filled the other two.

I'm happy to say my husband succeeded in fulfilling this challenge for me and took our challenge game to the next level.

How to Become a Sexy Wife

    Sexy, is how you feel about yourself. As women we need to own the word "Sexy". Whether slender, large, short or tall in statue. What ever we believe about ourselves our husband will too! Many women depend on their spouse to deem them sexy. The bible tells us we are fearfully and wonderfully made, every party of you.

    Therefore, if you believe in what God has done; you understand who you are. Being sexy is not just about our outward appearance. Although adorning ourselves with beautiful garments helps us feel and look sexy; "Sexy" is your mindset. How many women have you seen dressed poorly but convey "sexy?" You see them in the mall, at church, and even at work. Have you ever wondered why they capture your attention? It's not simply by what they are wearing, but their attitude. You silently acknowledge to yourself, "Who told her she looks sexy?" So, are you really referring to her outfit or her attitude? If you approach your husband with your head down and no confidence while wearing the nicest dress or lingerie. You've lost your sex appeal. When presenting yourself to your husband, hold your head high while you strut your stuff. Now you've got his undivided attention! Changing your attitude will help you become a sexy wife. Our husbands prefer nudity to fashion anyway. So here's my advice: First own it, become it, and then wear it! How many times have you heard "Take your clothes off?" Now that's sexy to our husbands!

Let's begin working on sexy. First start by conducting self-examination of your inner person. This means looking at your inner self, *not* visiting things from your past. This means confidence in your future. Understand, I don't deem myself an expert, but I do deem myself sexy. So let's move forward if you've struggled with becoming sexy.

According to the Webster's Dictionary "sexy" means: sexually suggestive or stimulating. Let's go a step further:

stimulating means to provoke. Therefore, when I think of provoking my husband. I simply tell my inner self, "It's provoking time!" Therefore, I purposely bring sexy out! So, my sensual attitude takes over. I plan an ambush, giving my husband absolutely no warning. No! I don't dress in lingerie or a skimpy skirt. It's just the way I walk into the room. I give him eye contact. It's like a flashing green light. If there's no response, I perform a little dance. Shake, shake, shake, shake, shake, shake, shake your bootie. Once you create a response or some form of stimulation, congratulations! You are deemed "sexy." Remember sexy is not a form of clothing. It's a stimulated act!!! So, each time you stimulate your husband, slap yourself on the rear end and say, "Where did you come from, you sexy thing!"

These Last Words

The beautiful, slender, well polished wife clears her throat. No more than 30 years old; the wife begins to give her testimony about having cancer. As she finds strength to speak, the tears well up in her eyes. Her husband reaches over, rubs her leg to comfort her and remind her that she isn't alone. Her lips part and she speaks. She shares with us how her doctors told her that she only had a few months to live. She begins to lose it and her husband, the same age as hers, picks up the testimony from where she leaves off. He describes long days and nights in the hospital, he shares how he felt, knowing that their young marriage was coming to an end due to the cancer taking over his wife's life. Together the tears from their eyes begin to fall as they hold each other's hands and look into one another's eyes. The wife says, "Life is so short. Enjoy it and stop thinking about the future. Live for today, enjoy each other, love each other, since you never know when your last day will come." The husband then adds, "I began to have a perfect peace after I realized that I did everything I could possibly do to show my wife how much I loved her before she was diagnosed. I knew that she was fully aware of how much she meant to me. Even though I was terribly saddened by the news, I didn't have any regrets."

Their testimony ends with the wife letting us know that, after going back and forth to the hospital, her doctors recently informed her that she was cancer free. As we all wipe the tears from the corners of our eyes, they look each other and smile with relief.

We become silent, because there is nothing to add. The hosts of the gathering take a minute to reflect and digest everything that was said, and then ask us all to write a letter to our spouse, imaging that the words on the page would be the last words our spouse would ever receive from us.

Gail Crowder and Other Sexy Wives

Here is my letter:

Dear Jelly Bean,

I dreamed of you all my life. You are my other half. I love you. At times, after a long hard day, I take refuge in the fact that I share the same bed with you, knowing that at the end of the day it's just going to be the two of us holding each other as the night passes into a new day.

Your hands' rubbing against my back at night soothes me like nothing on this earth. I love knowing that I can be anywhere on earth and, as long as you are there to hold my hand, my heart will always have comfort.

From the moment we met, our spirits spoke. I remember the day vividly. You were so well put together; you looked just like what I thought my husband was going to be. Once we started courting I connected with you in a way that I never connected with anyone before. You had authority that won my respect even though your words were gentle. You made me feel so special; I knew God was blessing me. Four years later, we were married and I still look at you and secretly smiles, because I know God continues to bless me. I admire you more than you could possibly know. We have experienced a lot, actually more than a lot. Even though we're only coming up on 8 months of marriage, sometimes it seems so difficult.

When I'm faced with the difficulties of marriage, at times I feel as though I'm drowning in my own grief. Not because I wish I wasn't married, or because of how you made me feel or what was said, but because I love you so much that I don't want us to experience the turbulence during the storm. I wish we could be perfect. But perfect is relative. During these times the Holy Spirit reminds me that in all actuality perfect is only in Jesus.

Therefore I constantly seek a place in Christ and retreat in the place of Christ within me where I can love you perfectly.

You deserve it. You deserve my best, not necessarily because of who you are or what you have done, but because you are God's gift to me. The first time we met our spirits spoke, and the Spirit of God continues to tell my spirit that our spirits are still speaking to this day. We just need to hush our flesh and spend more time listening and heeding. I'm blessed to know that, even though we may disagree, we're spiritually in sync.

Marriage is truly a mystery; the coming together of two making one is beyond words. Therefore, sometimes in silence is where we should rekindle the flame. Nothing in life is guaranteed, not even a last kiss or hug goodbye. Therefore, let me end with this:

For if I had to make the next few words my last to you, I would tell you that my love for you could never allow me to say goodbye, because you are my other half. I am totally me, in part because of you. As long as there is breath in my body I will love you more than you could ever possibly know. You are a good man and if you had to remember only one thing about me, always remember that I am totally in love with you.

What would your last words to your husband be?

Celebrating Our Engagement

It was a Friday afternoon when he met me at work to take me to the hotel where we were staying in mid-town Manhattan. I was so surprised when I walked into our room…a huge king-size bed and all the amenities to spoil a girl. I was completely in awe because he made the plans for our weekend, so every day was going to be a surprise for me. The hotel was absolutely beautiful; a place I had never been to before, but walked by quite often on my way to work. We were so excited; it was about one-and-a-half months since we got engaged and this weekend was all about us!

Once we got to our room, we took a shower, got dressed and headed out to dinner.

We ate at a quaint restaurant, not too far from where we were staying, where dinner was great. We had a good time, and afterwards, we walked around mid-town Manhattan talking about the plans for our future and how glad we were to be a couple.

We headed back to our room and that's when the real fun began….We undressed each other slowly, enjoying every moment of it; sometimes giggling in anticipation of what was about to take place. We climbed onto the bed and started kissing each other. He laid me down on the bed and started kissing all over my body, sending tingling sensations from my head to my toes….oooh. I was about to lose my mind with all those kisses and him nibbling on my behind (my favorite). Then it was my turn to reciprocate, and his gyrating let me know I was on the mark, pleasing him just as much as he had me. This was the discovery phase, because we learned places that brought about much pleasure. I had not experienced such ecstasy as I had that night. We took our time satisfying each other, making sure no body part was left untouched…smile. He entered me and we went to another place of delight; by the time we climaxed he said, "Baby Girl that was wonderful!" I'm glad we took our time, exploring and enjoying each other. Then we drifted off to sleep.

Saturday morning we woke up, and before he left to go to

work he ordered breakfast via room service for me. How darling and sweet he was to make sure I had something to eat; I truly enjoyed the food and the atmosphere. I drifted off to sleep again, totally content. Our room was great; I still couldn't believe I was there!! Eventually I got myself together and met him at his job; the plan for the evening was to see a Broadway play, "The Tap Dance Kid." It was wonderful; the performance of the actors was just breathtaking. I felt I could relate to everything that was going on in the play. The props we were so realistic; my mouth was open the whole time, marveling at how they brought New York City to life. We had another romantic dinner at Victor's Café, where we had seafood paella (his favorite) and sangria. Walking around Manhattan is the best; you never get tired of seeing the sights, no matter how long you work and/or live there.

Our lovemaking Saturday night was awesome. We fully enjoyed ourselves as we took our time since we realized this was our last night at the hotel. We wanted to soak up every minute...long kisses, more caressing, playing footsie and further exploring our bodies. When we were finished we went to sleep, spent--with smiles on our faces--as we spooned. It was absolutely wonderful (it reminded me of "Pretty Woman" scene...smile).

Sunday morning we woke up knowing this was it for the weekend. What a wonderful way to celebrate our engagement. We had breakfast (room service) and the thought of making love one more time crossed our minds, but we knew we had to get ready for work (we both worked at the same department store at the time). We did not want to go but knew we had to leave and get back to reality…

Foreplay

𝒯he sun hadn't come up when I heard his alarm clock. He has to be at work early. I felt his kiss on my neck- warm and a little wet. My entire body woke up. I reached up to hug him and pull him closer; I wanted to feel more. He whispered, "I love you" and as if it were a dream, I fell back to sleep. Hours later, when my alarm went off, I remembered how nice his kiss felt. I was in a good mood as I got ready for work.

The office was busy from the minute I got there and it continued until lunch. I wasn't going to answer the phone, but I thought "one more call", before I get something to eat. His voice took me back to the kiss I'd felt earlier. The tension in my body melted as we spoke. He talked about an important meeting and asked how my day was going. With my usual comments and a well placed joke about my boss, we shared a few laughs. He promised he'd be home early, but said he had to go. I sighed, but it was ok, since I was going to lunch. Later he sent me a text, "I luv U & 2nite imma finish wht I strtd." The feeling was back. I couldn't wait to get home.

Before I could put my purse down, I noticed lights in the kitchen and the dog out of her crate. I said, "Hello?" He answered, "Told you I'd be home early!" as he came out of the kitchen. I put the rest of my things down and we met at the kitchen door. He hugged me like he hadn't seen me in weeks. His arms felt so good around me. Then I felt his kiss again, first on my neck, then my cheek, then my lips. He pulled away, "Dinner will be ready in a few, and I made spaghetti." I asked where our son was, he said he was at the neighbor's house. I then asked, "Why isn't the dog over there, too?" We both laughed.

I poured a glass of wine and kicked off my shoes while he stood at the stove. He looked taller, his shoulders more muscular than I remembered. He was so sexy. We both tried ignoring the obvious while he finished cooking. During dinner he talked and I daydreamed. We used to make love daily when we first got married. "You're not even listening to me, are you?" he said.

I was looking right at him, but he was right. I hadn't heard a word. I wanted him to push the dishes off the table, and take me right there on the table like they do on TV. I quickly thought, "I am not cleaning that mess up!" He must have heard me thinking or felt my heart racing. He took my hand and I followed him to our bedroom.

Later when I woke up, I was smiling. My smile disappeared when I reached for him. He wasn't there. Just then the bedroom door popped open. "You were sleeping, so I did the dishes and put the baby in bed." As if the entire day hadn't been enough, those words made me hot. I told him to lock the door and come back to bed.

Days like these don't happen enough, but the man could teach a class on foreplay.

First Encounter

My story begins in January, 1991, just after the new year began on a cold and windy Friday night. I was home,--not doing much just watching T.V.--when a girlfriend called to ask if I would go clubbing that night with her and her sister. I wasn't much of a party girl or clubber but decided to go, thinking it may be fun or at least I wouldn't be bored.

My friends picked me up about 9 that evening and we headed to a nightclub called the Classics, off Allentown Road. We arrived about 45 minutes later. The club was packed, the music was pumping and people were grooving doing their own "thang." We found a table, ordered our drinks and just chilled, listening to the music while looking out for a cute guy who any of us would find ok to dance with. As it goes with clubs, you can meet a lot of peculiar people, like the old guys around 40, who were trying to pick up someone my age (at 23) to party with and buy drinks. Eeww! They were almost old enough to be my parent. No way, that was just creepy. Then you had the really young ones, around 19-20, with fake IDs trying to pass for 21; loud and immature and then there were the guys who just look like trouble. You'd find a little of everything at a club.

My friends and I talked for a while, danced a little with a few guys, but no one interesting seem to come along. It had gotten pretty smoky in the club, since there wasn't a separate smoking or no-smoking section, and I needed some fresh air. So I walked to one of the exits outside. Just before I reached the door I heard this guy call out to me, making some comment on how cute I was. I turned around and there he was: a 6 foot, well-built brown-skinned brother leaning against the wall, checking out the ladies, hoping for some attention, I'm sure. So I walked over slowly, feeling nervous, thinking it should be ok. I am usually not this daring, but heck-- one time won't hurt. When I had reached the area where he was standing, we went through brief intros, and he asked me if was by myself. I said that I was here with friends and asked him the same.

He said that he and some of his buddies were on weekend leave and wanted to have a good time. So I asked him where was he on leave from; and he said Quantico Marine Base.

We talked for a few minutes more. Then one of his buddies needed him for something and he asked me wait there, and said that he'd be right back. As he walked away I was checking him out; he had a cute tight butt and I liked the way he walked. I waited for a few minutes, and then realized that my friends might miss me, since I'd been gone for a while. Shortly after, he came back and I explained that I needed to go find my friends. He asked for my number and I said I'd think about it. Then he said he would probably be back here next week, if I thought I could come back and hang out. I left to find my friends--which I did--and then we went home. The following weekend we did come back to the club. He was there, although I didn't see him until we were about ready to leave. We talked some and I gave him my number. We talked on the phone a couple of times that week. He seemed like a nice guy, someone who may be worthwhile dating. I thought. The following weekend my girlfriend and I went to Quantico to hang out at a local club near the base. There was about six of us who went to hang out that night. I was nervous and shy at first, because this was third time I had been out to a club three weeks in a row. I was really out of my comfort zone but I was drawn to this guy I had met. We had a good time; we laughed, talked, danced and enjoyed each other's company, even though this was new to me. There was something about this guy that I liked. This was really cool but scary all at once, because I have never really liked someone this fast. I thought if I were to go all the way with someone he would be it right now. After partying at the club that night, we went back to the base to continue the party. We had to be snuck into the barracks, because outside visitors weren't allowed after a certain time. Now you know I was really way past my comfort zone, but it was very exciting. I had never done anything like it in my life. We all hung for a little while. Then the group broke off into couples, each going their separate ways.

Well, I guess I don't have to tell you that I ended up alone with this handsome Marine in his quarters. He turned on some music and we just chilled.

He enjoyed talking to me about the things I liked, didn't like, about how my day was--stuff like that and not like most guys that I met. Most of them only wanted one thing right off the bat: to see how quickly they could get the panties.

I knew he was interested in that way, but he was a gentleman, and he put no pressure on the issue. It wasn't long before we shifted from conversation to slow dancing in the small barracks room and things got a little hot, but I didn't mind. Yep, that's right; I was ready to go past second base all the way home.

So our wonderful evening was progressing nicely until we heard footsteps in the hallway. We quickly got to his bed which was the top bunk, and his bunkmate came in the room a few moments later. We were on the bunk being really quiet and still, so his bunkmate wouldn't know I was there. I had to hold my breath for almost a minute. I am glad his roommate was there only long enough to pick up something and go. I was really scared, because I knew that, if we were caught, my tail would be in some serious hot water. After he left we both let out a huge sigh of relief and then laughed about the whole thing. We did pick up where we had left off earlier and had a really good time. He made the night truly special and wonderful for me--something I had never quite experienced in that way before. He took his time to make sure I was comfortable, before taking care of his needs and desires.

My girlfriend and I caught up later to go home, since it was really late (about 2 am) and we had at least an hour's drive to get there. So the guys escorted us off the base using some back road and then we headed home.

Over the next several weeks my girlfriend and I took turns driving to the base to see our sexy chocolate military men or to pick them up and bring them back to our side of town. We talked constantly on the phone, almost every day, for hours--sometimes till I fell asleep on the phone and he would tell me to get off and get some sleep.

After five months of us dating he proposed to me. Then two

months later we got married at the courthouse. We've been married for 19 years and have two wonderful kids.

Rewind

"How did we get here?" Sharice Longings thought to herself as she sat across from her impeccably dressed husband, Alex. She sat there trying to reconstruct all the events which had led up to this day….and when she looked into his eyes a thrilling tingle ran from the nape of her neck down to the end of her spine. It was as if his eyes were a camcorder playing back one of the numerous times that Alex had driven her over the edge of desire, to that sweet spot, the place that both her mind and body loved to visit and never return from. Before she realized it, her breathing pattern had quickened, her nipples were erect and a sound all too familiar to Alex was coming out of her mouth….."Oooohhhh!"   Sharice seductively moaned while licking her lips. Her arm reached over to him as if on automatic pilot and she traced his lips with her finger. Alex caressed her hand and slowly began to kiss and lick her finger. She closed her eyes, threw her head back and began to sway in the chair….."MMMMMMMMM" "MMMMMM Baby, that's nice." Sharice moaned. She could feel herself becoming more aroused. Her body always responded intensely to Alex's touch…..even if she was angry with him. She could never deny what she was feeling deep within her. Quickly she stood up and unbuttoned the top two buttons of her blouse, exposing the new blood-red lace demi-cup, before passionately kissing him.   Alex swiftly maneuvered around the table without breaking their lip-lock and began tracing her shapely silhouette and prolonging their sweet tongue dance for what seemed like minutes. His mesmerizing scent engulfed her as they melted together on top of the table. They were in the sweet spot together now as Alex's body responded to her touch. He savored feeling Sharice's body quivering against his. He lifted her up and began serenading her, "Annnnnticipation...anticipating your every mooooove… annnnticipation...anticipating what we're gonna do! Whew!" slow dancing to their song. Sharice instinctively wrapped her long velvety legs around his hips as they continued their public foreplay.

Sharice's moaning grew to a fever pitch as their arousal was growing together. Alex danced them across the room to a large black leather chair and he lowered himself down into it with Sharice writhing in his lap. She eagerly unbuttoned his trousers and reached inside. "Yeah, Baby, that's what I'm talkin' 'bout" Sharice whispered, as she seductively slid down the front of Alex's body, ensuring continual contact with his body until she was locked in face to face with her hidden target. She licked her lips as she unwrapped the tip of his package. As Alex braced himself for the pleasure that was coming, he let out a deep "Ooohhhhh Baby, do that thang you do." Her mouth enveloped him and they were lost in their own world…..only to be interrupted by screeching chair wheels on the hardwood floor and several throats clearing at the same time. "UH UM! UH UM! Mr. and Mrs. Longings!" we heard, from both men and women sitting in the room. Sharice froze in motion and looked up into the eyes of the legal team at Feathermen, Taylor and Lloyd. Mrs. Featherman stuttered, "Mmmmmrs. Loooongings, will you still need our sssservices?" "You are still seeking a dddddivorce…right?" Sharice and Alex were suddenly jolted back to reality. They were looking at the different face; some shocked, some ashamed, and some aroused but all with blushing cheeks and mouths agape. One secretary had covered her eyes with her hands but was peeking sheepishly between the fingers. When the action ended, she instantly excused herself to the restroom. Another secretary sat entranced, staring at

Alex's crotch, with her right index finger in her mouth, sucking and licking it as if it were a lollipop. Mr. Taylor, her boss, had to touch her on the shoulder to break her concentration and bring her back from her fantasy. She jumped and left the room quickly after smiling at the law firm's newest client, Dr. Sharice Longings. Alex proudly rewrapped his package and lovingly assisted Sharice to her feet. Another quick survey of the room caused brief eye contact between Alex and Mr. Taylor, a senior partner at the firm, who smiled and gave a "you the man" nod of approval as he was exiting the conference room. Alex buttoned Sharice's blouse while she smoothed her hair back into place. His hands lightly brushed her breasts and Sharice leaned into his body again, purring like a kitten. They gazed into each other's eyes and were immediately compelled to kiss once more. This time, Mrs. Featherman broke in quickly. "Excuse me, Dr. Longings, but we will have to reschedule this deposition for another date…This doesn't appear to be a good time for either of you! I will have my secretary call your office to reschedule." "You are SURE that you want to go through with this?!" Sharice meekly responded, "Yes Ma'am, I am sure that I want to continue the divorce proceedings. That will be a great idea. I'll look forward to the call." Mrs. Featherman reluctantly left the conference room, shaking her head in disbelief at what she had just witnessed, closing the door to shield any unsuspecting clients and workers walking down the corridor. Alex was still holding their bodies together in a firm embrace. "I'm sorry, Alex…I forgot where I was for a moment...I can't do this, we can't do this...I can't believe I just did THAT....HERE...with you...and we're about to get a divorce," Sharice nervously blurted out. Alex hushed her rambling by placing a single finger on her lips and said, "We may have forgotten where we are...but we have not forgotten who we are...You have not forgotten who you are...You are Mrs. Sharice Longings, my sweet and sexy wife of 15 years...We are One Flesh...Our bodies crave each other...We are still in sync. I don't want to divorce and I don't believe you want to either." Alex continued, "We are good together and very good for each other...I know that we have grown apart over the last two years." Sharice broke in, "I know it's all my fault...all that time away from you, doing my writing and research for my PhD...I guess I got a little too close to my faculty advisor...I allowed his voice to replace your voice and your influence on me. "Alex interrupted her saying, "I'm very proud of you and your accomplishments...When you grow, we grow; just know that I'm in this with you...I will ensure that all of your future dreams are taken into account while planning a future together." "Are you free tonight? We can have dinner so we can talk it out?" Sharice reluctantly declined saying, "I'm sorry Alex, but I have a prior commitment that I can't get out of...can I get a rain-check?" "Of course sweetie, you can have a rain-check or anything that your heart desires! Cause I believe that your heart desires me....MMMM, how sweet that sounds," Alex purred. Sharice lost her thoughts as she felt herself swaying back and forth while Alex maintained his firm embrace. Their bodies were gliding around the room, dancing again to music that wasn't playing. Sharice rested her head on Alex's strong chest and savored his scent as if it were the only thing keeping her alive. After a five minute mental trip down memory lane, they noticed several faces peeping through the door at them. Everyone who had recently left the conference room had returned to get a peek at part two, but to their disappointment this show was rated G. Mrs. Featherman stood looking bewildered and again walked away shaking her head. Alex and Sharice Longings walked out of the law firm together. Alex's face had a serene look upon it, while Sharice's looked very serious and somewhat confused. As he opened the door of his wife's Land Rover, Alex said, "I hope it rains soon." Sharice smiled at him and replied, "I'll call you Sunday evening to make an appointment to talk." "My calendar is always free for you, Babe," Alex reassured her.

Sharice entered her bedroom door longing for a hot bubble bath and a long nap. She wrestled to clear her mind and to rekindle the excitement and anticipation of going out on her first date with another man since she was a freshman in college. The masquerade party tonight was the perfect atmosphere for her to let her hair down. She reviewed the pictures that Stewart had forwarded to her Blackberry. The feeling that she had met Stewart before continued to haunt her, as she dozed off to sleep. Stewart's voice spoke to her during her entire nap and he seemed to be promoting the relationship with Alex, which perplexed her.

When she awoke from the nap, she was confused about whether or not to proceed with her date with Stewart tonight. As she dressed in her purple princess gown, she relived her afternoon escapades with Alex, and found herself surprisingly aroused. Sharice began to labor over whether to shower again so that she wouldn't smell like sex. She remembered that Alex had once told her that most men can smell when a woman is aroused and Sharice didn't want to chance giving Stewart the wrong signals on their first date. She quickly disrobed and showered, lathering her body with her favorite scent…Alex's favorite scent, Passionfruit Mango. Her mind began to linger on Alex and before she knew it…she was masturbating. After the shower, Sharice tried to compose herself and refocus on what she previously thought would be an exciting experience…a first date with a new man. She began to hear the words that Alex had stated earlier, about how she remembered who she was…Mrs. Sharice Longings. Mrs. Sharice Longings was jolted from her daydream, dressed in her princess costume with a sexy mask, by her doorbell. Could this be her Knight in Shining Armor? She answered the door with butterflies in her stomach. She hadn't felt like this about any man except Alex. Why was she so nervous? This was a new beginning and this Stewart was Fine!

Stewart stepped through the door dressed as none other than a Knight in Shining Armor. "How ironic is this?"

Sharice whispered to herself. "Looks like he's wearing some sort of suit of muscles under it." Sharice continued to talk to herself. Stewart began to talk about the evening he had planned and Sharice tried to listen but she couldn't focus. She kept thinking about Alex, longing to see Alex. Sharice slowly removed her mask and sat in her chair with a look of defeat on her face. Stewart walked over to her, as if to console her and asked, "Is there anything I can do to help?" Sharice began to sob to herself. She looked up into Stewart's eyes, who was being so supportive of her as she melted down. She began to apologize for her behavior, "I'm sorry Stewart, for the imposition but I can't accompany you to the party with a clear conscience, when my heart and mind are longing to be with someone else...I thought I was ready for this...but I'm not...I'm still very much in love with my husband, Alex." Stewart knelt down beside Sharice and looked her in the eyes. Again, Sharice felt that she knew this man. "You are a very understanding man, and you deserve a woman who can focus her undivided attention on you," she said. Stewart whispered, "I think I've found her again!" Stewart stood up and removed the full-faced professional latex mask. To her astonishment and pleasure....Alex stood before her. Sharice ran to her man and kissed him as if she would never see him again. Alex carried his beautiful princess bride to the bedroom and they consummated their new relationship as husband and wife.

The next morning, Alex and Sharice awoke and thanked God for a second chance at loving each other. They talked to each other openly for the first time in years. They were naked and unashamed.

www.ingramcontent.com/pod-product-compliance
Lightning Source LLC
Chambersburg PA
CBHW060503110426
42738CB00055B/2611